DICTIONARY
bass grooves

BY SEAN MALONE

To access audio visit:
www.halleonard.com/mylibrary

Enter Code
3923-6777-4409-7952

Cover photos courtesy of Ampeg

ISBN 978-0-7935-8964-7

HAL•LEONARD®
CORPORATION
7777 W. BLUEMOUND RD. P.O. BOX 13819 MILWAUKEE, WI 53213

Copyright © 1998 by HAL LEONARD CORPORATION
International Copyright Secured   All Rights Reserved

No part of this publication may be reproduced in any form or by any means
without the prior written permission of the Publisher.

Visit Hal Leonard Online at
www.halleonard.com

ABOUT THE AUTHOR

Sean Malone has a B.A. in Composition and M.M. in Music Theory from the University of South Florida. He has performed and recorded extensively in North America and Europe on bass and Chapman Stick. He has had interviews and reviews of his recordings in magazines from North America, Europe, Japan, and Israel, including *Bass Player, Bass Frontiers, Guitar and Bass, Guitarist, Creem, Guitar Player,* and many others.

Sean has dozens of recordings to his credit including *Focus* by Cynic (RoadRunner), *Guitars That Rule the World Volume 2* (Metal Blade), *Working Man: A Tribute to Rush* (Magna Carta), *Bass Talk 5* (HotWire), *Under the Red and White Sky* and *The Closing of the Pale Blue Eyes* by John Wesley (CNR/Arcade), *Combination* by Todd Grubbs (Apollon International), *Notes from the Underground* (Guitar World), and his first solo CDs *Gordian Knot* (Sensory) and *Cortlandt* (AudioImage). He has performed, taught, and recorded with artists such as Mike Portnoy, Trey Gunn, Reeves Gabrels, John Myung, and Gary Willis. Sean has also taught at the National Guitar Summer Workshop in Connecticut and has written several articles for *Bass Frontiers Magazine.*

Sean currently lives in Eugene, Oregon, where he continues his writing, session work, and music theory research.

ACKNOWLEDGMENTS

Thanks to:
All at Hal Leonard, DR Strings, Ampeg, and Bill Mason for the ear and the input.

Special thanks to the musicians whose expertise, talents, and advice made the audio examples possible: Bob Bunin—guitar, Steve Connelly—guitar and pedal steel, Jack Owen—guitar, Sean Reinert—drums, Glenn Snelwar—guitar, Jim Studnicki—guitar, and Ed Woltil—guitar.

Recorded at Hitmakers Studio, Sulphur Springs, Florida. Recorded by Bill Mason, mixed by Phil A. Delphia
Mastered at the Springs Theater by John Stephan.

CONTENTS

INTRODUCTION

Bassists are often expected to be musical chameleons who are familiar with many different styles of music. Having knowledge of styles prepares you for almost any musical situation; a well-rounded bassist is an invaluable asset to producers and recording studios. However, you don't need to be a full-time session bassist to feel a need to aquaint yourself with different styles of music. The enjoyment of playing music is augmented when you draw from a diverse palate of musical influences, be it in the recording studio or a practice room.

The purpose of this book is to introduce you to a wide variety of musical styles and to explore the role of the bass within them. The concept behind this collection is to provide concise, hands-on examples which act as models that can be applied in a more far-reaching manner to the particular style you are interested in. Whether you are trying to expand your musical resources, or just explore other styles, this book can serve as a resource—a *Dictionary of Bass Grooves*.

What is a Groove?

The term *groove* means many things to many people, but there is an underlying thread which connects them all: the "locked-in" feeling between a bassist and the rest of the rhythm section. The term is used as a noun (e.g. That's a great funk *groove*.), and also as a verb (e.g. This songs needs to *groove* better). So groove is something we *perceive,* and something we *do.* The word groove is meant to describe anything that's regular and steady, from a rhythmically complex and driving funk groove, to a slow and lilting country and western groove. As long as it's tight, it *grooves.*

Style vs. Groove

In order to organize the grooves in this book, decisions as to what category they belong to where based on *style.* You can't really separate style from groove, but as you'll see, some of the characteristics of the grooves depend on style for their identity. For example, a salsa groove has well-defined characteristics in and of itself, independent of the context of the music. One can play a salsa groove in salsa music, or apply the groove to rock, funk, jazz, etc. On the other hand, the progressive rock example doesn't really "groove" at all; rather, it's a sample of rhythms, textures, and harmony that you might expect to find in progressive rock.

Learning Styles

If we are afforded the luxury of time, repeated listening and exposure to music helps to subconsciously build our musical vocabulary. Having a large palette of stylistic interests is not only personally satisfying, but can be professionally rewarding as well. If, however, a last minute call comes for a country session, and you've never played country before, it is essential to be able to zero in on what *makes* it country, or heavy metal, or bossa nova, etc. The *harmony, technique* and *tones* descriptions for each example do just that: they identify features of the music that contribute to the style.

Format

Dictionary of Bass Grooves was designed to expose the reader to the distinguishing characteristics of a wide variety of styles. This book is not meant to be taken as an exhaustive survey, nor is it bassist or band specific (except in the case of James Jamerson). The musical examples attempt to emulate each particular style, with idiomatic playing and compositional techniques.

Dictionary of Bass Grooves is divided into main categories, which are further divided into sub-categories. Each section contains:

1. Musical characteristics such as harmony, rhythm, etc.;

2. Some of the techniques employed in performing them;

3. Descriptions of the bass tones used by the players;

4. A list of players who are noted within the style;

5. A recorded audio example of the style;

You are encouraged to play along with the examples so you can immediately get a feel for the different grooves. The symbols that appear with numbers by the written examples correspond to the audio track listing. All examples are written for the four-string bass.

ROCK/POP

By the time Alan Freed coined the term "rock 'n' roll", a revolution in popular music had already begun. Rhythm and blues had been transformed into a high energy mixture of drums, piano, guitar, and bass that took the youth of the U.S. by storm. The music had an irrepressible pulse that launched countless dance crazes like the swim, the jerk, and the mashed potato. Rhythm and pulse are the name of the game when it comes to rock, and they are vital elements to all of the styles in this book. The term "rock 'n' roll" is still in common usage, but it is more often meant to describe the music of the fifties and early sixties. Today, the generic term "rock" is applied to a very wide spectrum of styles and sub-styles, which are all considered popular (pop) music.

The bassist's presence in popular music is as varied as the music itself. Bass guitar technology evolved with the music, allowing basslines to come to the forefront in recordings and performances. With the advent of synthesizers, new sounds and textures were explored, sometimes replacing the bassist altogether. What all of the styles of rock and pop music seem to have in common is a driving, locked-in rhythm section that supports the rest of the ensemble. Sometimes the bassist was given more room to explore, as in the case of progressive rock. Other times the bassist stayed in the pocket in a more supportive role, as in southern rock. Either way, the bass is part of the foundation.

This section of the book has the most variety under one category. There's no single "rock groove", or "pop groove", so here is where style plays a large part in differentiating the examples. When reading this section, pay close attention to what the styles have in common, and then eventually how they evolve and become varied. You will notice throughout hese grooves that even when a new "style" emerges, it often borrows heavily from something in the past.

1950s Rock 'n' Roll

The rock 'n' roll music of the 1950s heavily emphasized the rhythm section, often consisting of drums, bass and piano, with the guitar eventually emerging as an important contributor to rhythm and lead. The acoustic bass was prevalent, and played with a very percussive style, contributing to the overall groove of the rhythm section.

Harmony:

Fifties rock 'n' roll centered around dominant seventh and minor seventh chords, employing the major, Mixolydian and minor modes. Diminished passing chords were utilized occasionally for transition. Bassists often outlined chord tones in a texture similar to a walking bassline, which created an undercurrent of motion, while at the same time supporting the groove.

Technique:

An upright was the bass of choice, since at that time there really wasn't much to choose from. Bassists not only used the standard *pizzicato* technique of using two fingers to pluck the strings—they sometimes cupped their hand and used it to play with a percussive slap. You can imitate this technique on an electric bass by having an exaggerated downstroke with your fingers, simultaneously "striking" and plucking the string. But remember: this was done to make the bass louder and may damage a speaker with today's amplified electric basses. You might also try weaving a small cloth at the bridge of your bass to mimic a dull, thuddy sound.

Tones:

Since recording techniques were in their infancy in the 1950s, the bass is often difficult to hear. The common practice of recording an entire group was with only one microphone, and the bassist had to play as loud as possible just to be heard over the drums and other instruments. The sound was usually boomy, but had a very percussive quality as the large wooden body of the instrument moved a lot of air.

FEATURES
Driving rhythm
Bass lines outlining the harmony
Walking bass-style texture
Dominant and minor seventh chords
Percussive pizzicato technique

BASSISTS
Bill Black
Arthur Blackman
Norman Brown
Joe Mauldin
Gary Morrison

◆1 1950s Rock 'n' Roll

1960s Rock

FEATURES
More melodic bass lines
Independent bass lines
Introduction of various modes
Distant-related keys
Bass was more present in the mix

BASSISTS
Jack Bruce
John Entwistle
Paul McCartney
Noel Redding
Bill Wyman

Rock music of the 1960s quickly evolved with the advent of improved recording techniques as well as advancements in electric instruments. Players became well known individually and in groups, instead of the singer always getting the spotlight. The electric bass had arrived and redefined its presence in the groove.

Harmony:

The expanded harmony of sixties rock was an extension of chord progressions and key relationships from the previous decade. There was an introduction of modal use such as Lydian and Phrygian, distant-related keys (signatures that were more than one accidental different), and increased melodic independence. The music was slowly gaining as much importance as the vocalists and soloists it supported.

Technique:

Using a pick was popular, which was in part influenced by guitarists playing bass; it was considered a bass *guitar.* Fingers were also used which produce a mellower tone.

Tones:

Technology was rapidly advancing in the areas of amplification, recording equipment, and instruments. The bass was definitely more present in mixes, though the tone was often thin. That was not always the rule, as in the case of the Beatles, with whom Paul McCartney recorded some of the most memorable and influential bass lines of all time.

◆ 1960s Rock

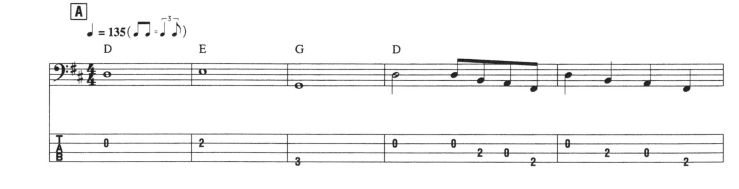

Hard Rock

FEATURES

Mixolydian and
pentatonic modes

Blues based harmony

Shadowed guitar riffs

Strong bass line pulse
with the drums

Full range of tones

BASSISTS

Michael Anthony

Pat Badger

Robert DeLeo

John Paul Jones

Gene Simmons

Hard rock is one of the evolutions of rock 'n' roll. Bands such as Led Zeppelin, Kiss, and Van Halen borrowed from influences such as blues and rock, and turned up the volume in the 1970s to create a heavier form of popular music. Hard rock brought about many innovations in technique and composition, as players were becoming famous not only for the band they played in, but for their virtuosic talents as well. There is a wide variety of hard rock bands, which harbor an even wider variety of styles. The bass was still part of the anchor, but began to venture out from its supportive role.

Harmony:

Hard rock saw a return to blues-based harmony at times, utilizing the blues scale as well as the Mixolydian and pentatonic modes. The tritone (an interval of three whole steps) was added to this vocabulary, and some groups employed the harmonic minor and Phrygian mode to create a more exotic sound.

Technique:

The pick was popular in hard rock though there were many fingerstyle players as well. The bass was more present in the mix, but was mainly supportive, often shadowing guitar riffs. Bass lines were a large part of the energy of a group, providing a strong pulse in conjunction with the drums.

Tones:

Bass tones were varied—from loud, distorted full-bodied sounds to small, thin, and midrange-oriented sounds. There was at times a "louder-is-better" mentality, sacrificing good tone for volume.

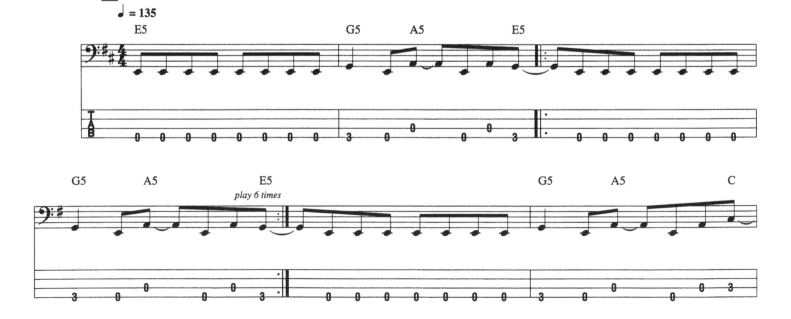

❸ Hard Rock

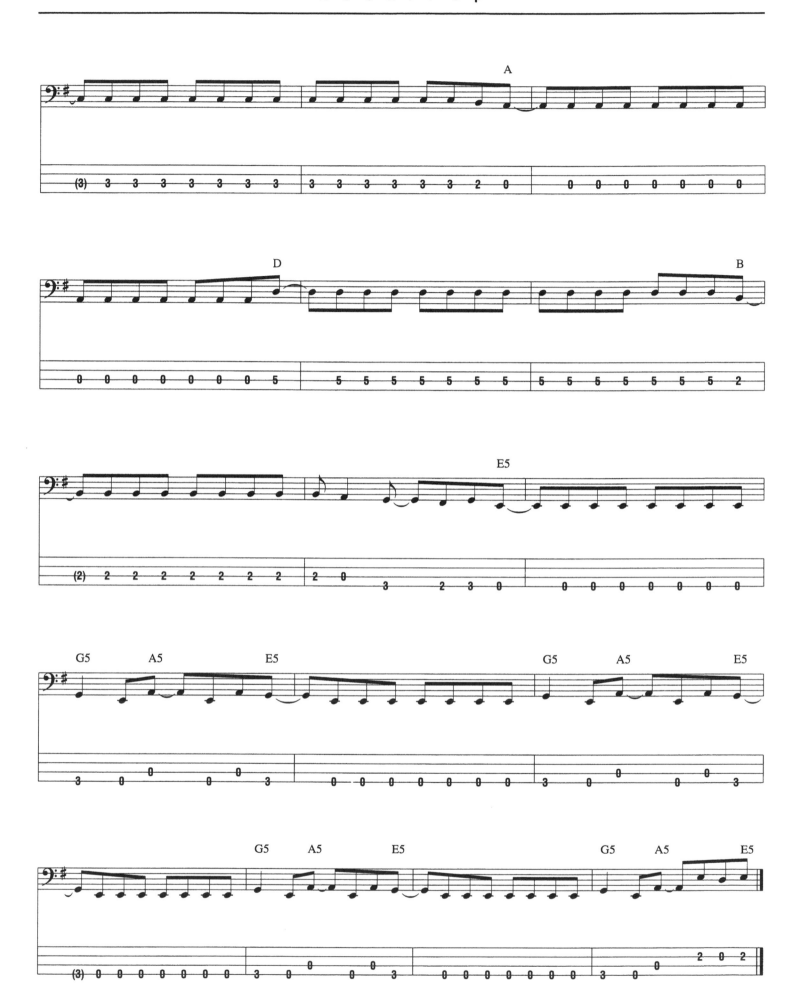

FEATURES

Bass joining
the guitar on riffs

Simple harmony

Pentatonic modes

Supportive, simplified
grooves

Gritty tone

BASSISTS

Harvey Arnold

Andy McKinney

Berry Oakley

Leon Wilkeson

Allen Woody

Southern Rock

Southern rock is a combination of hard rock and some elements of country and blues, all with a southern sensibility. Groups like the Marshall Tucker Band, Lynyrd Skynard, and the Outlaws popularized this style of music, incorporating slide guitars and a heavy dose of southern pride. The heyday for Southern rock was the mid-1960s through the 1970s in the Southeastern U.S. This style of music is still very popular today, though there seem to be fewer bands that are purely "Southern rock" bands.

Harmony:

Southern rock utilizes both major and minor scales and chords as well as major and minor pentatonic modes for soloing. Bass lines often join in with the guitar, playing riffs as well as holding down the groove with supportive, root-oriented parts. Chord progressions are largely key-oriented and repetitive.

Technique:

Finger and pick technique were both utilized.

Sounds:

The bass guitar didn't get a lot of attention in Southern rock. The tones often emphasize a lot of midrange, especially if the player used a pick. Some bassists often had a gritty sound—with a touch of distortion or fuzz—often times because of overloaded amps.

◆ Southern Rock

FEATURES

Extended song formats

Changing time signatures

Melodic bass lines

Unconventional playing techniques

Wide variety of bass effects

BASSISTS

Geddy Lee

Tony Levin

Christ Squire

Roger Waters

John Wetton

Progressive Rock

The term "progressive" is not easy to define when it comes to a style of music. We often have a notion of what it implies, but fall short of a clear-cut definition. From the 1960s onward, every decade produced "progressive" musicians. Bands like King Crimson, Genesis, Yes, Rush, and Gentle Giant played music that wasn't necessarily suited for mainstream radio or chart-topping record sales, due in large part to long and complicated songs that were challenging to the listener. What all progressive bands have in common is that they are all vastly different, and that they continue to try and push the envelope of musicianship and what is considered "rock 'n' roll."

Harmony:

A steadfast rule of progressive rock is that there are no rules. Harmony can wander all over the place—anywhere from Renaissance modality to free improvisation. There seems to be an attempt in most progressive rock to pack in as much music as possible. It's not uncommon to encounter songs of twenty minutes or more in length, virtuosic playing, odd time signatures, and extended solos. The scope of this book prevents an example that illustrates all of these characteristics completely, but listen to the many different sections and how various textures are expressed in each one.

Technique:

Since the nature of progressive rock was one of exploration, many new ways of approaching technique were investigated. The bass was a more melodic instrument at times, with a pick being used to play notes in the high register. Some bassists played instruments with multiple necks, either with a fretted/fretless combination, or a bass/guitar combination. Tony Levin's introduction of the Chapman Stick® (an instrument that has a range similar to a piano, played only by tapping on the strings) and more recently his Funk Fingers™ (shortened drumsticks attached to the first and second fingers that are used to strike the strings) have expanded the practices of conventional technique.

Tones:

Since progressive rock recordings span so much time, the sounds employed by bassists were contingent on the current state of technology and instrument making. As extraordinary as the explorations of new song forms, grooves, and harmony, so too were the inventive sounds in which they were expressed. Effects such as distortion, phasers, delays, and the Mutron™ brought the bass more to the forefront. The tone of the bass was sometimes gritty and thin, especially in the hands of bassists who were known to take solos. Other bassists preferred a softer, more languid tone which was well suited for flowing, melodic bass lines.

◆⑤ Progressive Rock

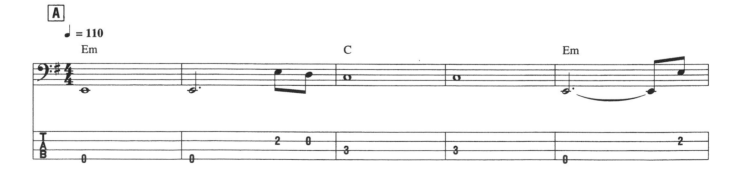

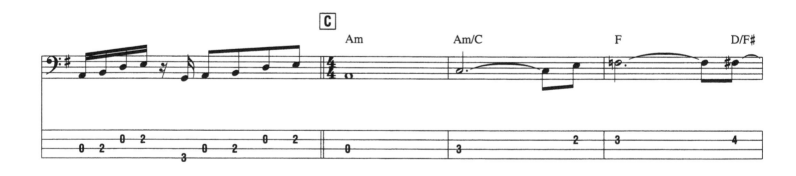

FEATURES

Distant-related harmony

Pick vs. fingers

Bass effects

Dynamic contrast

Supportive and
melodic bass lines

BASSISTS

Jeff Ament

D'Arcy

Mike Gordon

Mike Mills

Chris Novoselic

Alternative Rock

Alternative rock is a term that more accurately describes what the music *isn't* rather than what it is. Simply put, it is a style of music that purposely avoids mainstream pop formulas, targeting a social group that is dissatisfied with the corporate aspects of radio and popular music. There is a lot of diversity in alternative music—everything from dissonant, angry "grunge," to introspective spoken word. Alternative exploded in the nineties from the Northwest and thrives today, though the inclusion of alternative artists into the genre is malleable due to constantly changing criteria and mutable popular opinion from the underground.

Harmony:

Though at times repetitive and simple, alternative rock has provided some harmonic innovations, denying the expectations of generic top 40 harmony. The pentatonic modes are still popular, and chord voicings are often power chords versus fully voiced harmony. There is often a lot of dynamic contrast (loud and soft) as well as an emphasis on riffs. Alternative rock takes chances harmonically, utilizing distant-related key areas.

Technique:

Picking technique seems to be more popular than using finger technique, as the music is often aggressive in nature. A pick provides the means of playing harder and having a more cutting sound.

Sounds:

Along with harmonic innovations, alternative bass players have employed many different kinds of tones. All kinds of effects such as distortion, phaser, wah-wah, and delay are used to create textures that have never been heard before in "popular" music. Alternative bassists seem not only concerned with their actual bass part, but also with the overall tone and texture that the bass is providing.

◆6 Alternative Rock

* Key signature denotes E Phrygian.

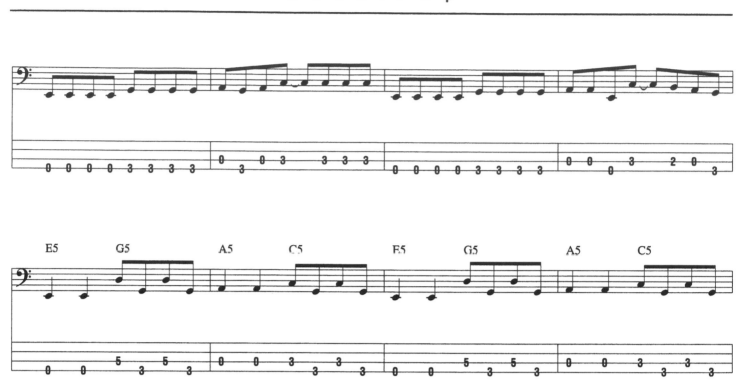

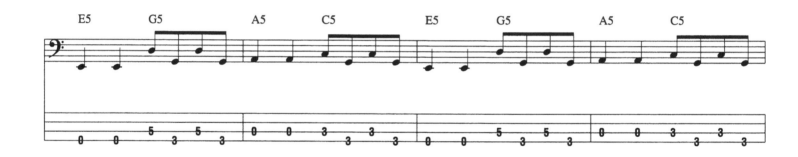

Punk Rock

Of all the revolutions that rock 'n' roll produced, none was as abrasive as punk rock. Punk began in the U.S. in New York City with artists such as The Ramones, Iggy Pop, and The New York Dolls. Despite being an American invention, punk's stronghold was in England with artists such as the Sex Pistols, The Clash, and the Buzzcocks. British punks were rebelling against the social, economic, and musical climate of the 1970s, emphasizing individuality and a do-it-yourself mentality. It was simple and powerful, making a high-energy statement that was easily accessible.

Harmony:

Pentatonic and Mixolydian modes as well as major and minor harmony are all found in punk rock. Modulation is rare, and most chords are closely related. There is a mixture of riffs and rhythm playing between guitar and bass, with the bass laying down simple, supportive grooves.

Technique:

Picking technique is used predominantly.

Tones:

Brash and up front in the mix to match the aggressiveness of the music, the bass was sometimes mildly distorted, often as the result of an overdriven amplifier. Tones were often thin and emphasized the midrange—due in part to recording technology at the time.

FEATURES
Aggressive picking technique
Pentatonic modes
Closely related chords
Brash tones
Simplified, supportive bass lines

BASSISTS
Fred Mills
Dee Dee Ramone
Derf Scratch
Garth Smith
Sid Vicious

7 ◆ Punk Rock

Disco

Disco lasted for about a decade in its prime, though it's currently enjoying a resurgence of interest. In the 1970s, artists such as The Bee Gees, Gloria Gaynor, The Village People, and KC & the Sunshine Band churned out hit after hit of energetic dance music. The impact of disco was immense and happened quickly, causing non-disco artists to quickly add the style to their repertoire to maintain their fan base. Just as quickly as it appeared, disco went back underground as discotheques closed and radio stations stopped playing the music. What was once the single most important craze in the seventies is now considered by many to be a musical stigma.

Harmony:

Though disco is often considered shallow and without message, the music still had some compositional depth to it. Dominant and minor seventh harmony provided a harmonic richness that augmented the emphasis on melody and groove. It was common to have string arrangements, and the advent of the synthesizer brought about unheard of textures.

Technique:

Disco marks the beginning of the bassist's struggle with the synthesizer. Performers were using the warm analog patches of the Moog synthesizer, often times eliminating the need for a bassist. Fingers were favored over picks, as there was some dexterity needed to perform the ever-present octave bass patterns.

Sounds:

Bass tones were often thin, but very present in the mix. Some effects were used in an effort to match analog synthesizer patches that were being created, such as chorus, flanger, and phaser.

FEATURES
Strong, dance-oriented grooves
Octave patterns
Seventh chord harmony
Bass effects
Fingers vs. picks

BASSISTS
Bernard Edwards
Richard Finch
Maurice Gibb
Nigel Harrison
Marshall Jones

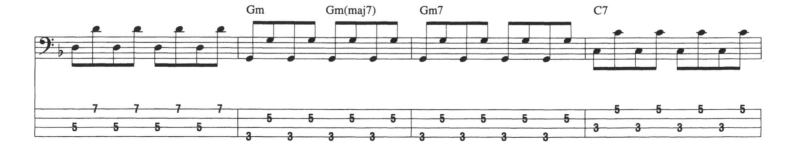

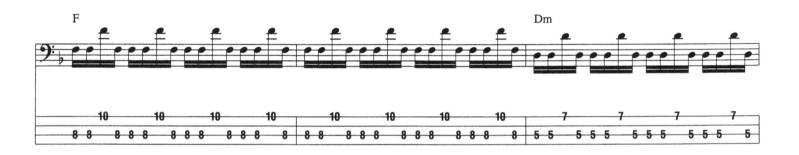

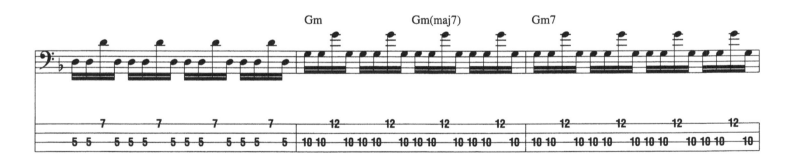

METAL

FEATURES

Fast tempos

Heavy, sometimes distorted tones

Pick and three-finger technique

Galloping bass lines

Detuning

BASSISTS

Geezer Butler

Cliff Burton

Steve Harris

Rudy Sarzo

Billy Sheehan

Metal music is an extension of rock and hard rock. Some bands of the late 1970s are considered to be metal bands in some form, but the genre as it's known today started to thrive in the early 1980s. Metal has many different subcategories, such as progressive, death, heavy, glam, thrash, hardcore, speed, black, technical, and grindcore to name a few. The evolution of metal music has brought about very fast tempos, blast beats, extreme technicality, crushingly heavy tones, and singing that ranges from operatic to brutal, guttural screaming. The appeal of metal is largely due to its high energy content and creates a parallel with the emergence of punk in the seventies. Metal was not only a reaction to the musical and social climate of the time, but continues to evolve today, producing some of the most brutally challenging music to listen to.

The bassist's role in metal music ranges from shadowing complex guitar riffs to creating a low, rumbling undercurrent that supports the singer and soloists. Metal bassists have made many advancements in technique, sometimes a result of the need to keep up with guitarists and drummers. Nonetheless, metal is an entire style of composition and performing unto itself, that has produced some of the greatest bassists playing today.

The examples in this section focus on progressive metal, heavy metal, and death metal. Though you might think that all three have a similar "sound," that is where the comparison stops. Progressive metal leans towards chops and technicality; heavy metal is a more "classic" metal sound which emphasizes a heavy texture versus demanding technique; and death metal is the most extreme evolution of metal music.

Heavy Metal

Heavy metal developed out of a need for an aggressive, faster, and more distorted kind of rock music. Earlier bands such as Black Sabbath, Motorhead, Saxon, Talus, and Deep Purple set the stage for today's metal bands with innovations in technique, guitar processing, harmony, melody, and rhythm. Lead guitarists began developing soloing techniques that had never been seen before, while rhythm guitarists were no longer just an extra player in the band—they were now creating accompaniment styles that became very involved and complex, as well as idiomatic to a myriad of styles and genres. Bassists, however, still were not very much in the spotlight, often times settling for playing exactly what the guitarists were playing, though a few bassists stood out with their melodic bass lines and athletic technique.

Harmony:

Heavy metal relied firmly on major and minor pentatonic scales and modes, as well as on the more exotic sounding harmonic minor and Phrygian mode. The tritone was used heavily for its particular sound in chords and riffs, and there was generally no restriction to the type of chords used.

Technique:

Bassists used their fingers and picks, developing their technique in order to keep up with fast tempos. Some bassists used three fingers on their picking hand which created a signature "gallop" to their bass lines.

Tones:

Heavy Metal bass tones are often very deep and full sounding. Distortion is often used to create an even heavier sound in combination with the guitars. The four string bass is still being used primarily, though it is sometimes detuned to create a deeper sound.

◆⑨ Heavy Metal

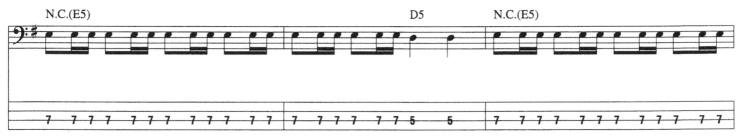

Progressive Metal

Progressive metal is an off-shoot of heavy metal which is distinguished by its extended song formats, changes in key and time signature, inclusion of keyboards, and varied instrumentation. It borrows from progressive rock in its grandiose themes and orchestrated textures, but differs in its faster tempos and heavy, distorted sounds. As in the case of progressive rock, it's difficult to define what makes it "progressive." Something that all progressive bands have in common is the desire to expand upon what has come before them—to write a new chapter in music and to discover more advanced ways of communicating their musical ideas. Progressive metal has a small but devoted audience made up mainly of musicians. Its popularity continues to grow in the underground scene.

Harmony:

Anything goes in progressive metal—from pure diatonic harmony, to exotic scales and modes. One thing that is consistent is that the harmony does not usually stay in one place for very long.

Technique:

Progressive bassists are often technically oriented players. Fingers are mostly used, though you'll occasionally find someone using a pick. Fingers allow more versatility than picking, which is needed to accommodate ambitious basslines.

Sounds:

Bass tones are usually deep and full-bodied, with occasional distortion for heaviness. Some effects are used, but done so sparingly, as the emphasis is on playing and technique rather than texture.

FEATURES
Changing time and key signatures
Technically challenging
Melodically independent
Unrestricted harmony
Finger technique

BASSISTS
Joe Dibiasc
Doug Keyser
John Myung
Peter Nordin
Joey Vera

◆ 10 Progressive Metal

C

Dm

B♭

Fade Out

Gm

Death Metal

Fast tempos

Three finger and double picking technique

Complex riffs

Scooped-out tones

Detuning

Steve DiGiorgio

Shane Embury

Chris Richards

Frank Watkins

Alex Webster

The following is a description of death metal by producer and engineer Scott Burns: "Dynamics are not a part of death metal; it's loud in the beginning, middle, and end. It's just sheer, guttural brutality—there is no singing involved." There isn't much to say that can more accurately describe this form of music, except that it is at the most extreme end of metal, and music in general. Though death metal is often maligned for its subject matter and on-stage antics, it remains as some of the most passionate and difficult music to play. Death metal has a strong international following, and though its popularity has already peaked, it's sure to reinvent itself as metal has over the last two decades.

Harmony:

Death metal has set its own standard for harmony employing the use of the tritone, distant related key areas, highly complex riffs, and extreme chromaticism. Diminished arpeggios and wholetone scales are often used as well.

Technique:

The pick is popular in death metal as well as fingerstyle, with three fingers often being used in order to articulate many notes at very fast tempos. Double picking is also popular, which seemingly doubles the amount of notes being played.

Tones:

Bass tones are deep and sometimes distorted with a very "scooped-out" equalizer setting (removing the midrange). Bassists also detune their four-string basses as much as a minor third or more to try and create as heavy a sound as possible.

⑪ Death Metal

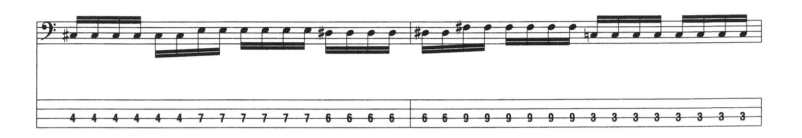

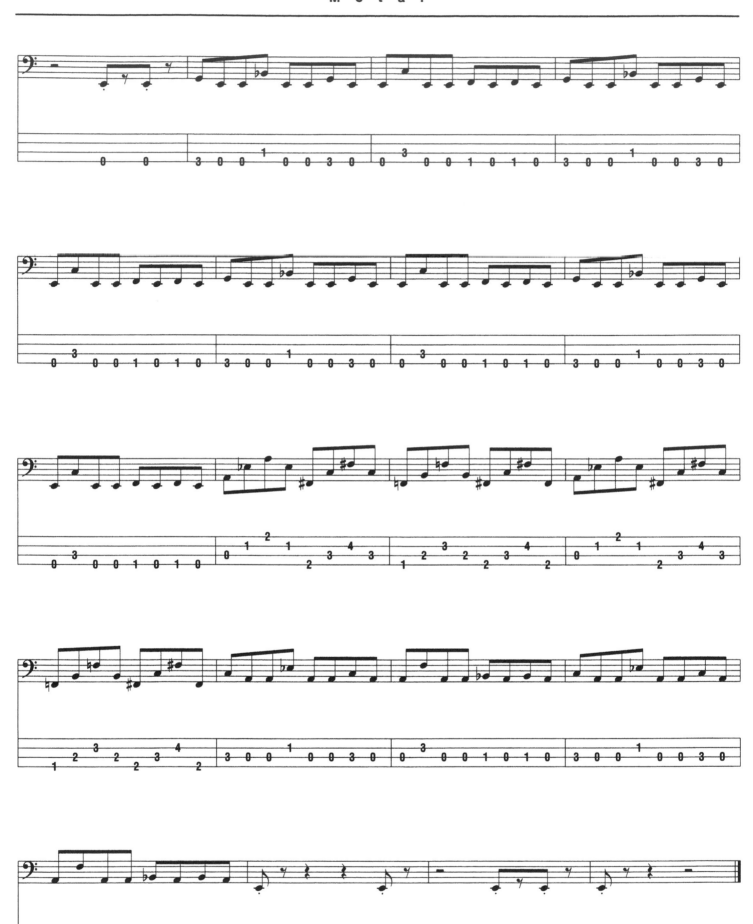

34

RHYTHM AND BLUES

Rhythm and blues combines elements of blues, gospel, jazz, boogie-woogie, and pop music with a strong backbeat and a deep groove. As the name implies, rhythm is the name of the game. R&B arose in black communities during the post-swing era (between 1945–1960), before the arrival of the Beatles. The term "rhythm and blues" was popularized in the late 1940s by *Billboard Magazine*, replacing the unfavored term "race music." R&B continues to evolve and is some of the most popular music in the United States, deserving of its own charts of record sales and airplay.

The examples in this section contain a shuffle feel, a ballad, and a groove in the style of a man who single-handedly defined the Motown sound—James Jamerson. The shuffle groove owes more to its feel than its choice of notes. Notice how the bassline is steady quarter notes that anchor the rhythmic accents of the drums. The ballad example emphasizes how the bass can have some melodic independence while still anchoring the band. The Motown example shows some signature figures of James Jamerson.

Harmony:

Major, dominant, and minor seventh chords were primarily used, with the emphasis on rhythm and melody. Scale choices ranged from major, minor, and pentatonic, in addition to the Mixolydian mode. It is not unusual to have many key changes to closely and distantly related key areas. The harmonic content of R&B is usually very rich, providing many possibilities of inversion (a note other than the root played by the bass) and melodicism for the bassist.

Technique:

Fingerstyle playing is predominant, though the development of slap and pop technique added a new dimension to R&B.

Tones:

Early R&B featured low, thuddy bass tones—especially the tones of James Jamerson. This added to the percussive and rhythmic feel of the bass in the mix. To duplicate this sound, try weaving some string or a small cloth at the bridge of your bass. Modern R&B features crystal-clear bass sounds due to state of the art recording technology and advancements in instrument design.

FEATURES

Deep grooves

Melodic bass lines

Rhythmically active, but supportive

Finger and thumbstyle

Dark, percussive tones

BASSISTS

Tommy Cogbill

James Jamerson

Jerry Jemmott

Chuck Rainey

Gerald Veasley

⬥12 Motown

◆13 R & B Shuffle

14 R & B Ballad

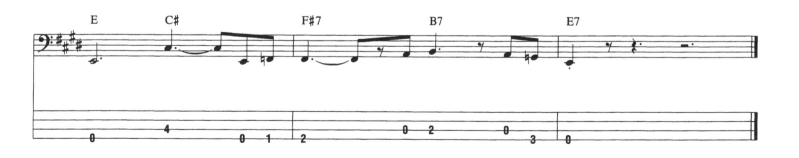

JAZZ

Jazz as we know it is a purely American art form, though its beginning was influenced by the blues and African slave work songs and spirituals. The heritage of African music is retained in jazz through its rhythmic elements and collective improvisation. Jazz is based on song forms which have a melody (sometimes called the head) supported by a chord progression. After the melody is performed, the form of the song is played continually (called choruses) and the harmonic structure is used for soloists to improvise over the "changes" (chords). The melody is then played again, signaling the end of the tune. Jazz songs that have become staples of performers over the decades are called standards, all of which embody chord progressions and melodies that are a part of a common vocabulary, defined by certain eras and performers.

The blues form—chords built on the tonic (I), subdominant (IV), and dominant (V) played in ten-, twelve-, to sixteen-measure lengths—was a holdover from blues and gospel music. It can simultaneously be the easiest and the most difficult progression to play over, as decades of musicians have tried to expand the blues progression to its limits. Each of the three chords can be "substituted" with other chords, implying a different harmony and creating tension in the music. As the years rolled on, composers and soloists continued to add to the harmonic vocabulary, eventually leading to the bebop revolution.

Bebop was music for musicians—characterized by harmonic complexity, fast tempos, rhythmic dexterity, and seldom yielded to popular taste. Led by saxophonist Charlie Parker in the 1940s, bebop became the music of choice in New York night clubs, producing some of the world's greatest jazz musicians.

In stark contrast to bebop is modal jazz. This type of jazz is based on linear and modal qualities of improvisation and composition, rather than chordal and harmonic concepts. Tunes were much slower and less technically demanding, creating a very open sound that allowed improvisers a lot of room to experiment with exotic scales. Modal jazz presents its own challenge of maintaining interesting basslines and accompaniment, due to the sparse amount of harmonic material.

The following three examples employ the walking bass technique—a steady pulse of quarter notes that supports the harmony but provides linear independence. Jazz music is often expressed in chord charts rather than written out basslines. The bassist must be aware of what notes are in the chords and connect them with a line of varied contour, usually playing chord tones on beats 1 and 3. There are many exceptions to that description, and exposure to many different bassists will help you absorb the style.

Harmony:

Jazz harmony is based primarily on seventh chords of every quality. Modern jazz more often employs extensions such as the 9th, 11th, and 13th, which give the bassist more chord tone choices to use in the bassline. The difficulty of a tune is defined not so much by the types of chords used, but how quickly and numerously they change in the composition.

Technique:

Fingers are used exclusively to provide a warm, percussive tone.

Tones:

The acoustic bass was, and still is, the bass of choice among purists. Even electric basses are equalized to provide the warmest tone possible. The bass functions as the pulse of the rhythm section, and plays the ultimate supportive role.

◆15 Jazz Blues

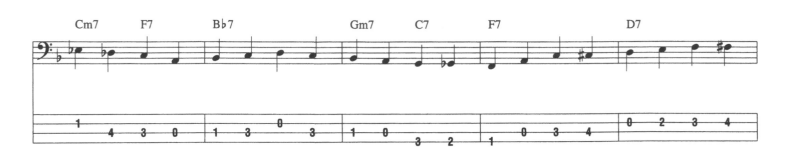

🔷16 Bebop

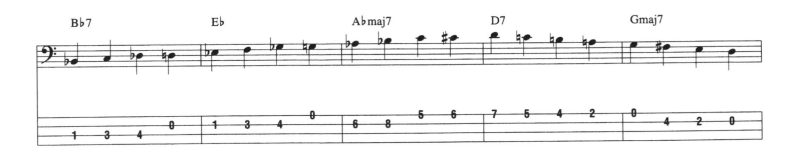

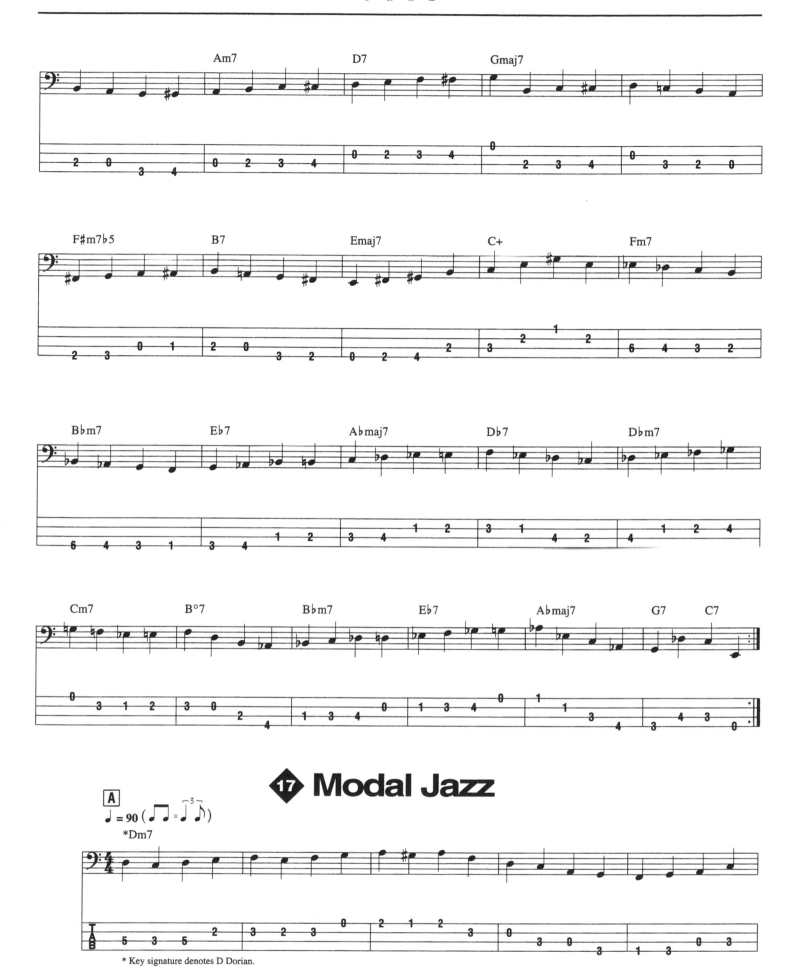

◆ 17 Modal Jazz

*Key signature denotes D Dorian.

Fusion

Jazz fusion is an umbrella term which encompasses many styles, but is traditionally thought of as a combination of rock and jazz. Spearheaded in the 1970s by Weather Report, fusion became more accessible to a large amount of listeners. This was no longer the traditional swing jazz that preceded it, but a combination of high energy rhythms and electric instrumentation. However, fusion still pays a large debt to the jazz masters of the past by retaining compositional depth and instrumental dexterity.

Harmony:

Anything goes, including seventh chords and extensions (9th, 11th, 13th), and all types of exotic and synthetic modes and scales, such as the octatonic scale and modes of the melodic minor scale.

Technique:

Fingers are used predominantly, though you will find those who use a pick occasionally. Some players utilize the slap and pop technique as well.

Sounds:

Tones vary from warm, fretless bass to deep and percussive fretted bass. The five- and six-string basses have come to prominence in the last decade, and can often be heard with a little bit of chorus or flange.

FEATURES
Combination of rock and jazz
Dissonant harmony
Technically challenging
Four-, five-, and six-string basses
Fretted and fretless

BASSISTS
Stanley Clark
Jimmy Haslip
Jaco Pastorius
John Pattitucci
Gary Willis

18 Fusion

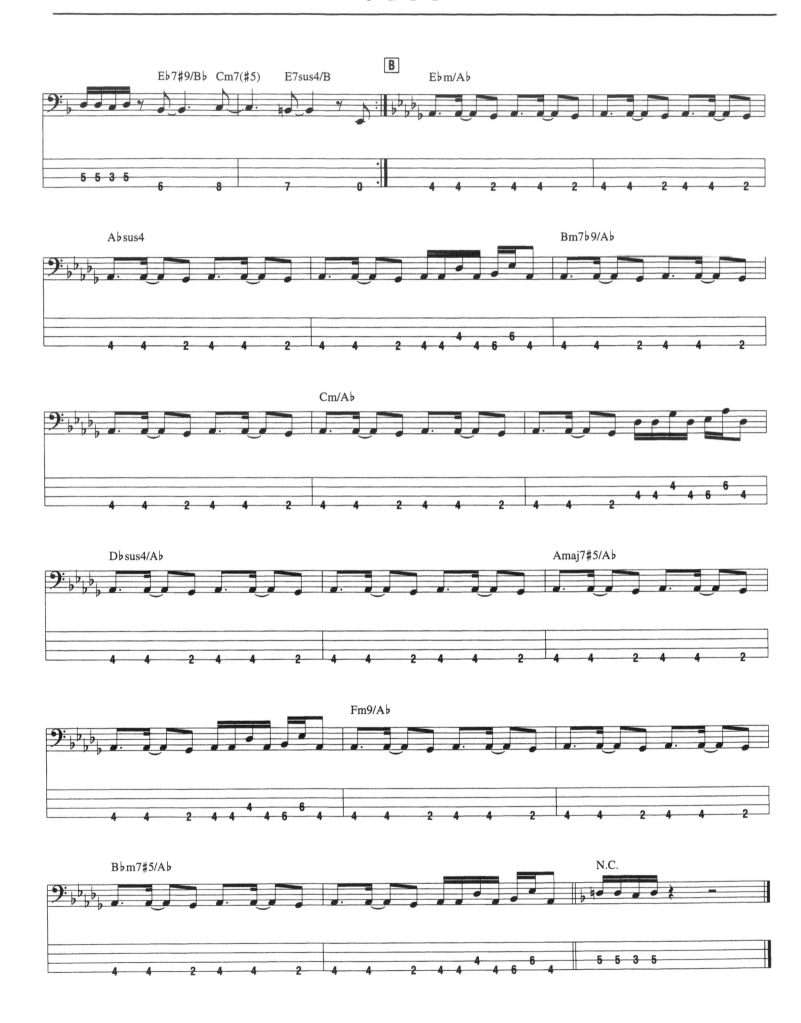

AFRO-CUBAN

Afro-Cuban music (also called Latin music) has a long and rich history rooted in the dance rhythms of Cuba, Brazil, Puerto Rico, and the Dominican Republic, that have been mixed with influences from Africa, Western Europe, the Caribbean, and the Americas. The generic term "Latin music" is often replaced with "salsa" (Spanish for *sauce*), and meant to encompass a wide variety of rhythms and grooves.

Two important elements of salsa are the *clave* and *tumbao*. The *clave* (Spanish for *key*) is the rhythmic foundation of salsa. It comes in two basic forms: the 2:3 son clave, and the 3:2 son clave.

FEATURES

2:3 or 3:2 Clave

Heavily Syncopated

Unrestricted harmony

Repeated tumbao figures

Acoustic or electric bass

PLAYERS

Sal Cuevas

Juan Formell

Lincoln Goines

Andy Gonzales

Israel "Cachao" Lopez

This rhythm is always present in the music—either implied or explicitly played. There are variations of the clave, such as the rumba clave which displaces the last note in the "3" measure by an eighth note. Choosing between the 2:3 or the 3:2 clave depends greatly on the phrasing of the melody, and the interaction between the bass and percussion.

A *tumbao* traditionally refers to a repeated figure in the congas, but has also come to described any repeated bass figure as well. Bass tumbaos are often, but not always, heavily syncopated (emphasizing the weak part of the beat). Salsa is usually felt in 2 beats (cut time) and the last half of beat two in the bass is often tied to the next downbeat, anticipating the next chord change. This anticipation creates a lot of rhythmic variety when the piano or guitar waits until the following downbeat to change chords, adding to the overall polyrhythmic feel of the groove.

All of the audio examples for this section use the same chord progression so you can concentrate on the sometimes subtle differences between bass lines. A single displaced note or rhythm could mean an entirely different groove.

Harmony:

There are no restrictions to the harmonic make-up of Latin music. Salsa grooves can be applied to any music, and it has been the combination of latin rhythms with jazz harmonies that have brought this exciting music to a wider audience. "Cubop" was the name of an instrumental genre of the 1940s and 50s that merged bebop and Afro-Cuban music. The bass notes that anticipate the change of harmony often land on the root or fifth of the following chord.

Technique:

Finger technique prevails in Latin music, though there are many great examples of Afro-Cuban funk using the slap and pop technique as well. Traditionally, the bass is played with strong and rhythmic pizzicato.

Tones:

Many salsa bassists prefer the acoustic bass for its rhythmic quality, but often play electric uprights as well. The bass is very present in salsa and usually has a warm, round, and fat tone.

🔷19 Salsa

20 Cha-Cha

♦21 Afro-Cuban $\frac{6}{8}$

22 Bossa Nova

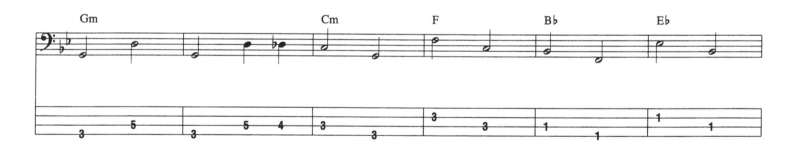

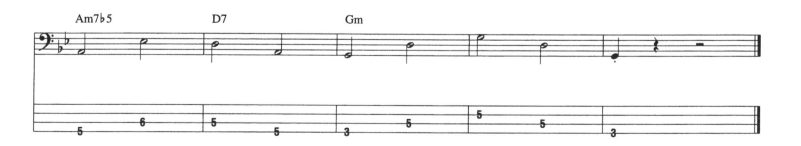

23 Samba

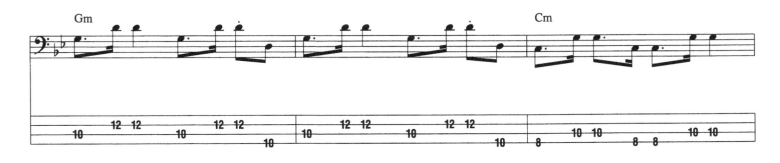

◆24 Rumba

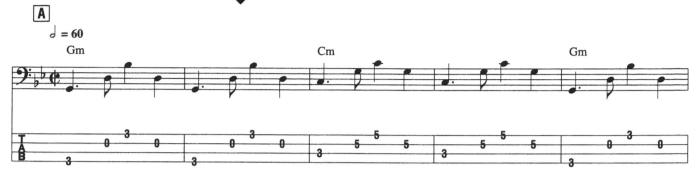

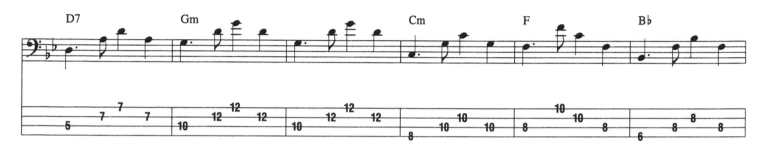

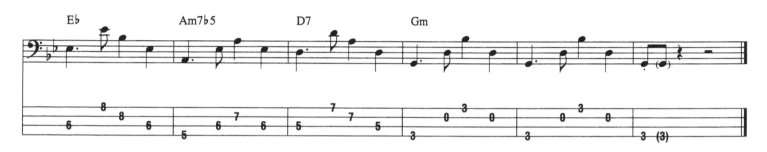

◆25 Mambo

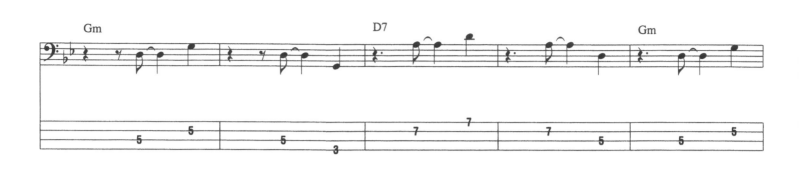

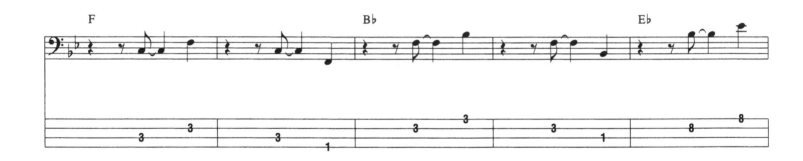

AFRO-CARIBBEAN

The music of the Caribbean has a rich and varied history. Each island has its own particular style or groove, and various subtle variations of each. The music is a melting pot of African rhythms and melodies, combined with Caribbean work songs that developed into many diverse styles. Each style has its own unique characteristics, and this section takes a look at three of them.

Reggae originated in the 1960s from the ghetto areas of Kingston, Jamaica. It is a mixture of Jamaican folk music with American R&B and dance music. Artists such as Bob Marley and the Wailers and Peter Tosh became recognized the world over. There was a practice with reggae recordings that involved using the same recorded groove for many different songs and singers. Once a song was discovered to be popular, producers would find other singers to perform different melodies over the same grooves, or "riddims." Reggae is characterized by emphasizing the off beats (beats 2 and 4) and strong bass hooks.

Soca is party music which originally emerged as a fusion of Indian and African rhythms—due largely in part to the strong Indian heritage of Trinidad. The name soca itself was a combination of soul and calypso, as was the music, which was heavily influenced by American R&B. Soca music has now evolved into the definitive indigenous musical form of the Eastern Caribbean. The music is part of the Caribbean culture that has spread throughout North America and Europe. Soca music emphasizes beat two, creating a strong syncopation that contributes to this very simple but deep groove.

Ska is a motley combination of local folk forms with calypso, R&B, swing, boogie woogie, early rock 'n' roll, and jazz. It was popularized in the 1960s but eventually fell out of favor in the Caribbean. It was more upbeat than reggae, soca, or dancehall music, but eventually slowed down, similar to the style of rock steady. During the late seventies, ska was fused with the high energy stylings of British punk rock, creating a synthesis of traditional Jamaican dance rhythms and the rebellious intensity of punk. Ska has become popular in the U.S. in the 1990s, particularly in the Northeast. Ska bass lines tend to be very active, melodic, and frenetic (like the rest of the music), often outlining the harmony.

Harmony:

Afro-Caribbean music uses predominantly major, minor, and seventh chords. Reggae and soca harmony is usually pretty narrow and repetitive. They are, after all, forms of dance music, with the emphasis more on the groove and the message. Basslines often used melodic patterns to fill in the sparse chord texture, utilizing pentatonic modes as well as major and minor scales.

Technique:

Fingerstyle technique is used mainly to help punctuate the rhythmic nature of Caribbean basslines. The use of octaves and other intervals require string skipping, which is easier to execute with fingers versus a pick.

Tones:

Bass tones are warm and round. There is some experimentation with effects such as chorus and flange, but for the most part, basses are equalized with low end and some midrange.

FEATURES
Mixture of Jamaican music and R&B
Melodic, independent bass lines
Pentatonic fills
Emphasis of the upbeat
Warm and round tone

BASSISTS
Aston Barret
Earl Falconer
Ian Lewis
P-Nut
Robbie Shakespeare

26 Reggae

27 Soca

28 Ska

COUNTRY

FEATURES

Simple, supportive
bass lines

Diatonic harmony

Fingers versus a pick

Round bass tone

Very tight
rhythm section

BASSISTS

David Hungate

Bob Moore

Ray Price

Cedric Rainwater

Allen Williams

Country music developed in part from string bands that date back to the American frontier. Instruments such as fiddle, banjo, guitar, mandolin, and autoharp were used to perform traditional fiddle tunes, southern folk songs, and popular nineteenth-century parlor songs. By the 1950s, country and western music became a popular form of entertainment and a strong seller in a burgeoning record industry. There were famous singers and instrumentalists that stayed rooted in the traditions of the past, while at the same time paving a road to the future.

Though country music is considered simple for the most part, it is an excellent example of how basslines should support the rest of the group. The bassist often plays half notes, emphasizing the tonic and dominant pitches. Country depends on a very tight and solid rhythm section, creating some of the deepest grooves in music today.

The first example in this section represents a more traditional country and western sound and feel; the second is a more modern, electric form of country that crosses the border of rock 'n' roll. Notice that the bass lines have similar characteristics on paper, but sound quite different in the context of their respective grooves.

Harmony:

Country harmony is very diatonic, as it often is supporting a vocalist or instrumentalist. Closely related keys and diatonic scales are used often, with occasional hints at the blues scale. Basslines are very supportive with little melodic movement, and have a tendency to shadow guitar riffs in modern country.

Technique:

Fingers are favored over a pick, though both are used. By muting with the palm of the hand, you can emulate a more acoustic bass sound.

Tones:

Some of the best production is found in country music. Warm, full-bodied, well-rounded bass sounds blend well with the rhythm section. Country session bassists often have a collection of basses they bring to the studio. Each one has a particular tone, and the producer might have a specific sound in mind for a song.

⬥29 Country Western

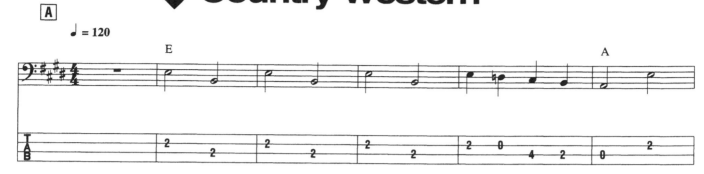

⬥30 Country Rock

BLUES

The origins of blues music can be traced back to African work songs and field hollers, as well as gospel, jug bands, jazz, and ragtime. Blues existed prior to the twentieth century, but wasn't called "blues" until the 1900s. Blues styles come in many forms: Delta, Piedmont, Chicago, jump, and Memphis to name a few. A defining characteristic of the blues that ties all of its variations together is the chord progression on which it's based: I, IV, and V. Blues music has two main components: the blues progression and the style in which it is played, which is usually named from the region where it originated.

The progression itself can be found in many styles of music, such as rock, pop, jazz, Caribbean, Afro-Cuban etc., and has been subject to many variations. The main structure remains intact, usually grouped within twelve measures—hence the moniker "12-bar blues." Blues artists consider this type of music a way of life, depicting the hard times they and others have fallen upon. If music is a universal language, then blues is a powerful dialect, spoken especially throughout the South.

The examples in this section represent two kinds of grooves—a laid-back, more traditional groove, and an upbeat blues/rock groove. The chord progression stays the same (I, IV, and V), with the first example playing a more traditional line that supports the harmony via chord tones. The second example is a more melodically active line that passes through chord tones, creating a strong sense of motion.

Harmony:

Blues is defined in large part by its harmony: the I, IV and V chords. These are usually dominant seventh chords, with their counterparts in minor used often as well. The Mixolydian and pentatonic scales are used, in addition to (and most importantly) the blues scale.

Technique:

Fingerstyle and picking technique are both widely used. Fingerstyle is best suited for active or tricky lines, and can provide more dynamic variety and greater expression. Picking technique is best suited for sharp and punctuated bass lines that need to cut through the rest of the group.

Tones:

Bass tones in blues music are often dark and gritty, though this is not always true. Since there are so many blues players out there, just about every tone imaginable has been used. Listeners often focus on the soloist and the singer rather than the rhythm section, so the bass doesn't often get much attention. However, the bass should have a full tone, as it may be the only instrument playing behind the soloist at times.

FEATURES

Chord progression based on I, IV, V

Mixolydian and pentatonic scales

10-, 12-, 14- and 16-bar forms

Styles based on region from which they came

Supportive bass lines

BASSISTS

Roscoe Beck

Willie Dixon

Duck Dunn

Karl Savareid

Tommy Shannon

31 Blues Shuffle

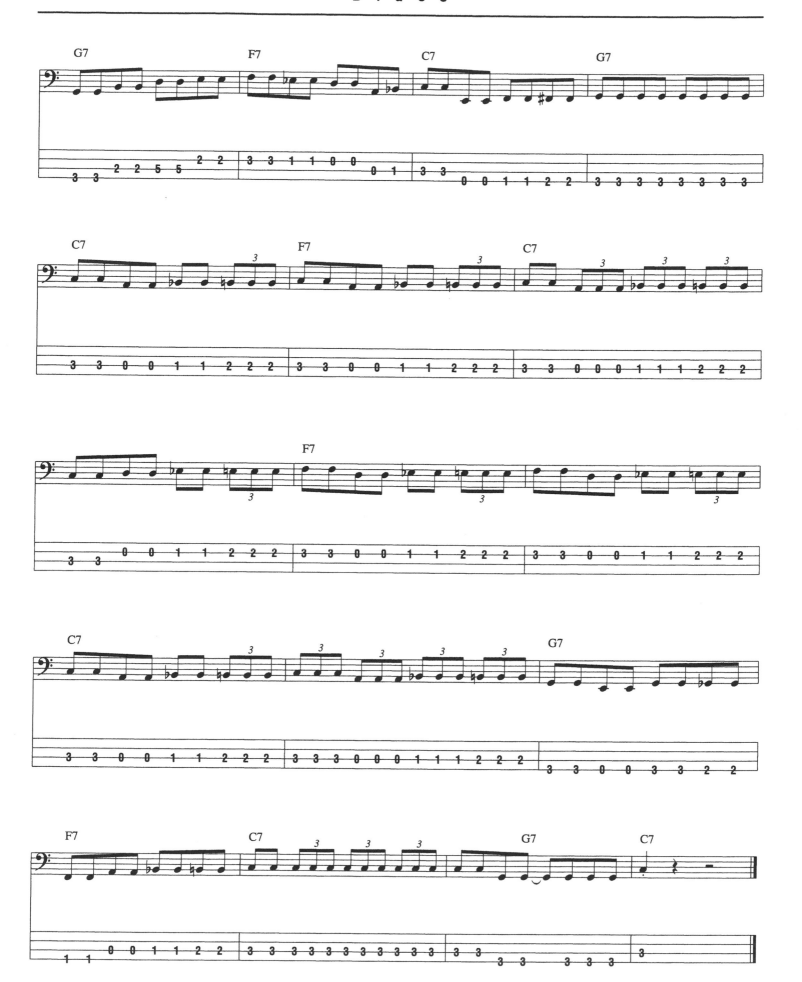

32 Blues Rock

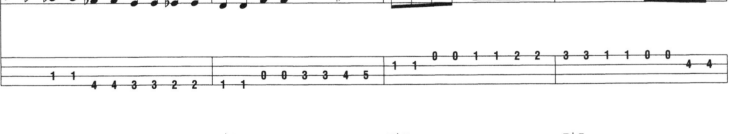

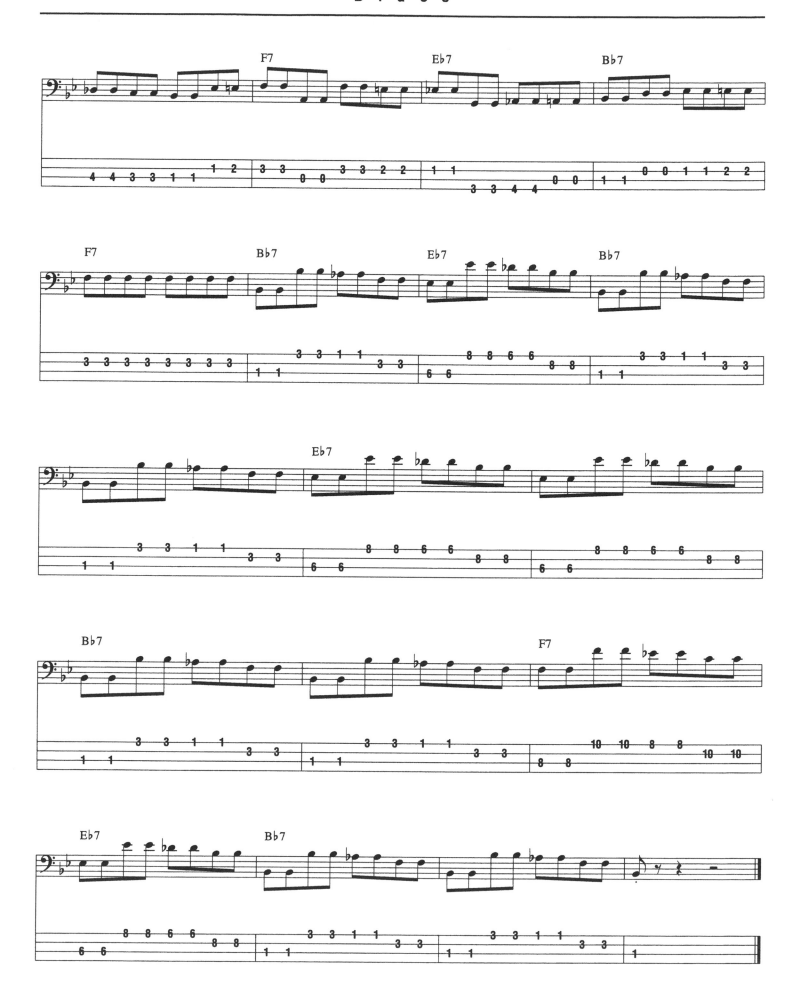

FUNK

FEATURES

Deep and heavy grooves

Fingerstyle and thumbstyle

Staccato rhythms

Mixolydian mode

Use of the Mutron

BASSISTS

Bootsy Collins

Flea

Larry Graham

Rocco Prestia

Victor Wooten

Funk is difficult to describe in words because it's not only a style of music—it's also a mentality, a sub-culture, and for some, a way of life. Funk peaked in the late 1970s, as a combination of just about every style of music—R&B, rock, jazz, soul, you name it. Funk absorbed its musical surroundings and preached a message of musical brotherhood. Early Funk bands like P-Funk, ConFunkShun, Kool and the Gang, and even the Average White Band promoted a party atmosphere at concerts, inviting the listeners to join in on the music making.

Funk is as popular today as it ever was and has seen decades of transition and metamorphosis. Disco was even considered an off-shoot of funk, due in part to the dance-heavy aspects of the grooves. Today, funk has crossed over the borders of a wide variety of music. There's acid jazz, "Hollywood" funk, funk-rock, old-school, and many more. Funk is a bass player's heaven.

Above all else, rhythm is the most important element of funk. Drums, percussion, and bass all contribute equally to the groove, and must be locked in and tight. Playing funk on bass comes in two: fingerstyle and thumbstyle. Fingerstyle technique creates a very percussive and rhythmic bassline, however there is no percussive "slapping" of the strings. The fingers are continuously moving, locking in with the subdivided beat (usually the sixteenth note). Left and right hand muting help to create staccato (short and accented) articulations. Fingerstyle funk can be very demanding on the picking hand, and requires a lot of relaxed technique and stamina.

Thumbstyle, or slap and pop, involves three main components:

1. Slapping the strings with the thumb of the picking hand.
2. Popping or plucking with the picking hand.
3. Muting with the fretting hand.

This technique produces very percussive and rhythmic bass lines that create a deep groove with the drums. The fretting hand also hammers notes at times, which can effectively double the amount of playable notes.

The two examples in this section—one a fingerstyle example, the other a thumbstyle example—utilize the same drum and accompaniment track so you can focus on the differences between the two techniques.

Harmony:

Funk utilizes a lot of dominant seventh harmony, as well as minor sevenths. There are at times blues-based influences with the use of the Blues, pentatonic, and major and minor scales. There isn't a great deal of modulation, and if there is it is usually to closely related keys. Funk features extended vamps, allowing soloists to improvise over the groove.

Technique:

Fingerstyle and thumbstyle are used. See the introduction to this section for a more detailed description.

Tones:

Funk recordings have documented some of the greatest bass tones of all time. Tones can be full and round for fingerstyle, or thin and trebly for thumbstyle. Bassists who play busy lines often have a strong midrange presence in their tones which allows you to hear the notes clearly. Effects like the Mutron helped define the seventies funk sound, and are becoming popular again.

◆33 Slap & Pop

◆34 Fingerstyle Funk

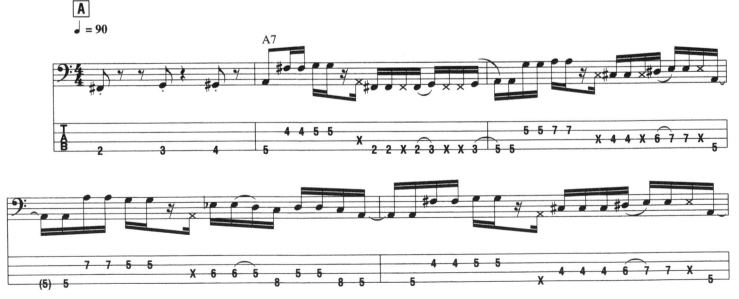

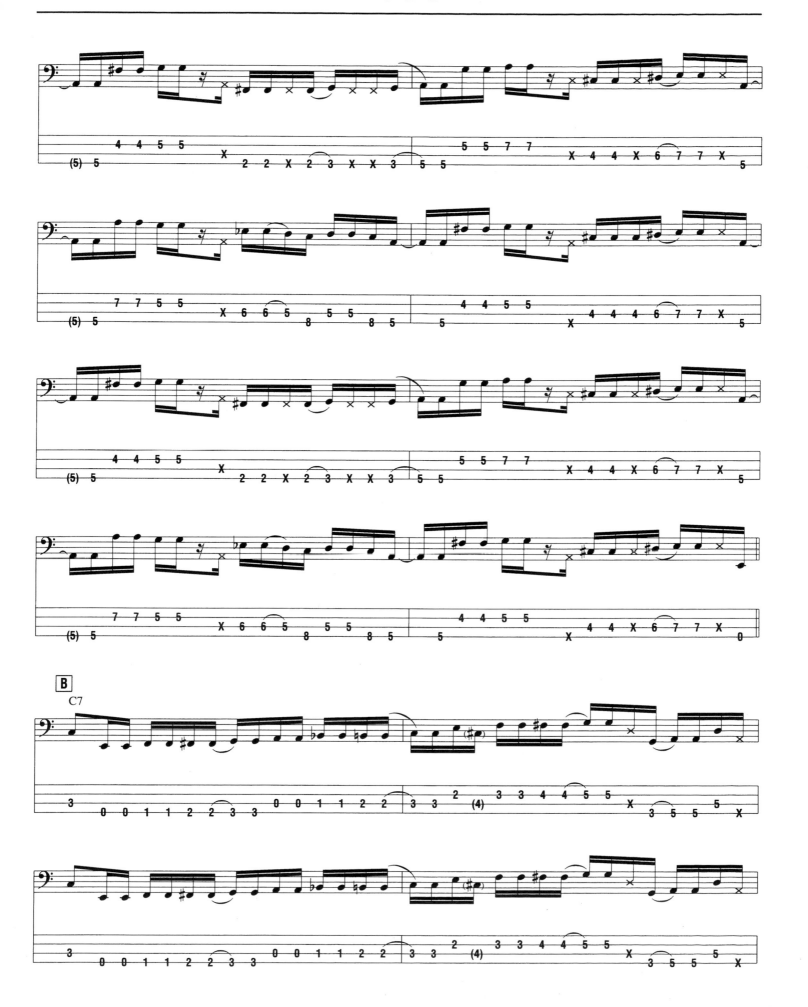

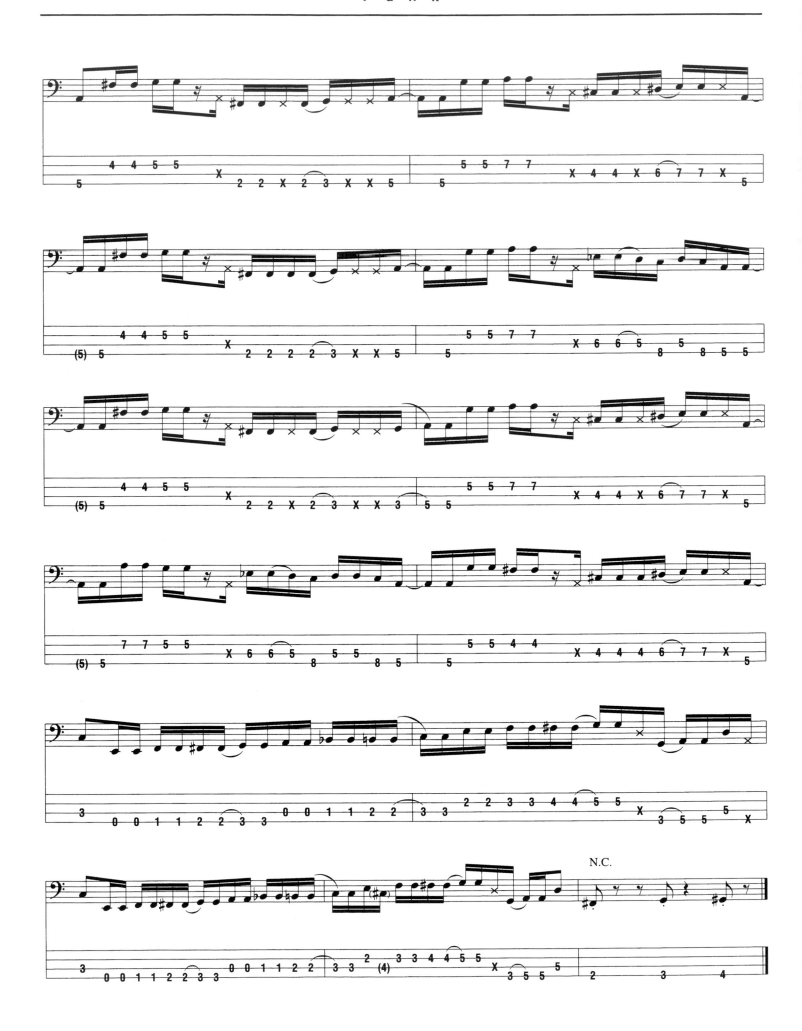